LITTLE BOOK OF COCKTAILS

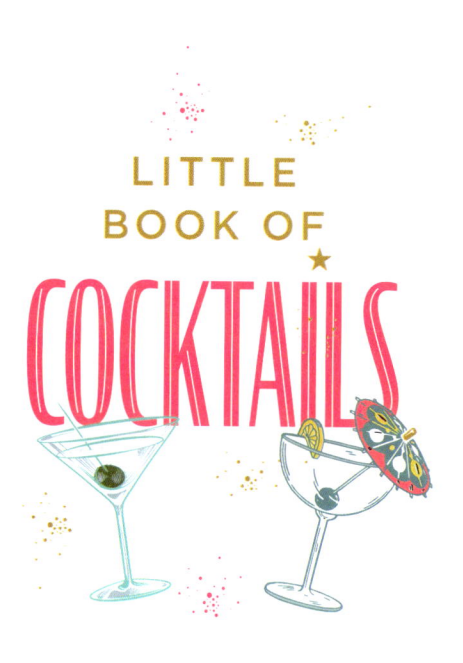

An exclusive edition for

ALLSORTED.

This edition first published in Great Britain in 2024
by Allsorted Ltd WD19 4BG U.K.

The publisher is not responsible for the outcome of any recipe you try from this book. You may not achieve the results desired due to variations in ingredients, typos, errors, omissions, or individual ability. You should always take care not to injure yourself or others on sharp knives or other cooking implements or to burn yourself or others while cooking. You should examine the contents of ingredients prior to preparation and consumption of these recipes in order to be fully aware of and to accurately advise others of the presence of substances which might provoke an adverse reaction in some consumers. Recipes in this book may not have been formally tested by us or for us and we do not provide any assurances nor accept any responsibility or liability with regard to their originality, efficacy, quality or safety.

This book contains information that may fall out of date and is intended only to education and entertain.

The publisher shall have no liability or responsibility to any person or entity regarding any loss or damage incurred or alleged to have occurred directly, or indirectly, by the information contained within this book.

This book is intended for adults only. Please drink responsibly.

All rights reserved. No part of this work may be reproduced in any form or by any means, electronic or mechanical, including photocopying, recording or by any information storage and retrieval system, without the prior written permission of the publisher.

© Susanna Geoghegan Gift Publishing

Author: Helen Vaux
Cover and concept design: Milestone Creative
Contents design: seagulls.net

ISBN 9781915902658

Printed in China

10 9 8 7 6 5 4 3 2 1

CONTENTS

Introduction 5

All about cocktails 6

Tools and glasses 12

Techniques and terms 15

Rum 18

Vodka 40

Gin 62

Whiskey 84

Brandy 106

Champagne, wine and bubbles 128

Tequila 140

Mocktails 148

Mixing notes 160

'The well-made cocktail is one of the most gracious of drinks. It pleases the senses.'

David A. Embury

INTRODUCTION

If you think cocktails are something only a flamboyant bartender can create, think again. Cocktails don't need to be complicated. They don't even need to be sophisticated. Yes, it helps to follow the measurements in the recipes correctly to get the best results, but if you don't, it's not the end of the world – you might end up with something even tastier! Cocktails are your chance to get creative at home (and save some money on bar bills).

This book covers the 'Big Five' spirits used in mixology: rum, gin, vodka, tequila and whiskey. Almost every cocktail contains one of these, but we've also thrown in some brandy recipes and others that use champagne and wine. Plus, if you fancy something non-alcoholic, you'll find a range of mocktail recipes that are just as delicious as their boozy counterparts.

Whether you've mixed a Margarita or two in your time or are a complete novice, this book will help you create classic cocktails, as well as some more unusual ones. All that's left to say is, let's get shaking and stirring!

ALL ABOUT COCKTAILS

ALL ABOUT COCKTAILS

WHAT IS A COCKTAIL?

A cocktail is a mixed drink that consists of a base spirit (such as vodka, rum, gin, tequila or whiskey) combined with various mixers and flavourings. These can include fruit juices, syrups, bitters, sodas and other spirits. Cocktails are often also garnished with fruits, herbs or spices to enhance their taste and make them look good.

Now, if we're getting serious, we need to talk about the differences between 'cocktails' and 'mixed drinks'. A mixed drink refers to any drink that contains two or more ingredients, typically alcohols. On the other hand, a cocktail contains specific proportions of alcohol, sweetener and mixer. For the sake of ease – and because it's such a lovely word – we're simply going to call all the drinks in this book 'cocktails' (even if they're technically 'mixed drinks' – are you still following?).

Cocktails are composed of three parts: the base, the modifier (or body) and the perfume.

- **Base:** This is the spirit that provides the drink's flavour and alcohol content.
- **Modifier:** This enhances the base spirit's flavour (for example, juice, vermouth or soda water).
- **Perfume:** This is a small dash of liqueur, bitters or syrup that completes the cocktail.

It's the blend of all three of these that gives every cocktail its unique flavour.

A BRIEF HISTORY OF COCKTAILS

Cocktails were originally inspired by the punches that were popular in Britain in the 18th century. These punches – served from a bowl – contained a mixture of spirits, fruit juice and sugar. The first mention of the word 'cocktail' was in a British newspaper in 1798 and the first proper definition of 'cocktail' appeared in an American newspaper in 1806. The definition described a cocktail as a potent concoction of spirits, bitters, water and sugar.

In the 19th century, the art of mixology began to flourish. Bartenders like Jerry Thomas, often considered the 'father of American mixology', published influential guides, including *How to Mix Drinks* (1862).

The early 20th century saw the Prohibition era in the United States (1920-1933), which actually boosted cocktail culture. With the sale of alcohol banned, 'speakeasies' popped up and cocktails became a way to mask the taste of inferior bootleg and homemade spirits. Post-Prohibition, cocktail culture continued to boom. The 1950s and 1960s marked the golden age of cocktails thanks to them being popularised by Hollywood and American pop culture. Glamorous movie stars were rarely seen out and about without a cocktail in hand.

Interest in cocktails waned in the late 20th century but they became popular again in the early 21st century, thanks to the emergence of artisanal ingredients and craft cocktails.

WHERE DOES THE WORD 'COCKTAIL' COME FROM?

There are three main theories:

1. It is a mispronunciation of the French word for 'eggcup': *coquetier* (pronounced 'cocktay'). This stems from the story that an apothecary in New Orleans in the 18th century served brandy mixed with bitters in eggcups.

2. In the 17th century, a horse with a docked tail was said to have a 'cock tail' and it came to mean an adulterated horse. Due to the link between horse racing and liquor, the word 'cock tail' started to also mean an adulterated spirit, i.e. one that had been mixed with something else.

3. It is derived from 'cock tailings', a term that refers to how tavern owners would combine the dregs ('tailings') of nearly empty barrels into a single mixture that they then sold off cheap. The tap on a barrel was called a 'cock'.

GARNISHES AND PRESENTATION

Cocktails are all about style and elegant presentation. As well as looking good, garnishes complement the flavour of the drink to give the drinker a more 'complete' experience.

Garnishes also let you change how your cocktail tastes to suit your own tastebuds. The most common garnishes are lemon and lime wedges placed on the edge of glasses. Their purpose is to let you regulate the level of acidity and sourness of the drink. If you prefer your cocktail to be sweet, ditch the citrus. If you like a tart, sour drink, you can squeeze in as much lemon and lime as you need to reach the taste you like.

Of course, garnishes don't need to be edible. Decorations can include things such as swizzle sticks, umbrellas, flags and straws – even pink plastic flamingos. It's your chance to have a bit of fun, especially with cocktails like the Piña Colada!

BUILD YOUR BAR

You don't need every spirit and ingredient under the sun unless you're planning to learn hundreds of recipes. Start with the ingredients for your favourite cocktails. You can't go wrong

ALL ABOUT COCKTAILS

by investing in a selection of the following:

- Spirits – a basic home bar should include a bottle of gin, vodka, rum, tequila and whiskey.
- Fruit juices.
- Simple syrup (see page 17).
- Bitters.
- Lemons and limes!

See 'tools and glasses' on pages 13-14 for a basic list of the essential equipment you'll need.

If you don't make cocktails regularly, you might end up with a cabinet of dusty bottles. Here's a quick guide to the shelf-life of spirits:

- Unopened liquor of all kinds will generally keep indefinitely if stored out of direct sunlight and at normal room temperature.
- Distilled spirits (e.g. whiskey and gin) don't become unsafe to use, but they may start to taste 'off' one to three years after opening.
- Liqueurs usually last for six months to a year after opening.
- Vermouths and other wine-based spirits need to be refrigerated and used within six to eight weeks.

TOOLS & GLASSES

TOOLS & GLASSES

You don't need fancy gadgets to create the recipes in this book, but it does help to have a few essential tools to hand. This will make your life easier and ensure you get the best out of the recipe.

THE BASICS

Jigger: Precision is key when you're mixing drinks. A jigger will ensure you measure all your ingredients precisely and get the right balance of flavours.

Cocktail shaker: For shaking at home, a traditional cobbler shaker is all you need. It consists of a metal container, cap and a built-in strainer.

Strainer: Even if your shaker has a built-in strainer, some recipes require you to 'double strain' the drink to make it as smooth as possible. A strainer is simply placed on top of the glass as you pour in the drink. A Hawthorne strainer is specifically used for fine straining.

Muddler: A muddle looks a bit like a long, thin pestle and pretty much does the same job. See 'Muddling' on page 16.

GLASSES

Official cocktail etiquette demands a particular glass for a particular drink. However, you don't need to follow the rules at home! Here are the glasses mentioned in this book:

Balloon – generous bowl for long cocktails over ice.

Champagne flute – long-stemmed with an elongated, slender bowl.

Collins – tall and slender, ideal for serving long drinks.

Coupe – a stemmed glass with a fairly round, shallow bowl with straight sides, unlike the V-shape of a martini glass.

Highball – ideal for long, tall drinks. (Not as tall as a Collins glass but interchangeable.)

Hurricane – similar in shape to a hurricane lamp.

Julep cup – a silver or tin cup in which mint juleps are traditionally served.

Lowball/Rocks/Old Fashioned – a short tumbler. (A Double Rocks/Double Old Fashioned glass is 60ml larger than the standard version.)

Martini – a long-stemmed, V-shaped glass with a wide rim.

Mixing glass – if you're not shaking a cocktail, you may need a mixing glass. Basically, this is a roomy and sturdy glass, often with a handy pouring spout.

Nick & Nora – a long-stemmed, high-sided inverted bowl shape with a narrow rim.

Poco Grande/Piña Colada glass – a large capacity, tulip-shaped glass. Similar to a hurricane glass but shallower and with a longer stem.

If you don't have the 'correct' glass, it really doesn't matter. Just use something of roughly the same size.

TECHNIQUES & TERMS

THE LITTLE BOOK OF COCKTAILS

As an amateur mixologist working in the confines of your own home (and probably without an audience), what are the techniques and terms that you need to know? Here are the key ones you'll come across in this book:

Dash – As careless as a dash sounds, in the cocktail world it's quite precise and is the equivalent of 0.9ml or 12 drops. But, really, an extra drop or two isn't the end of the world.

Straining – Traditional cocktail shakers have built-in strainers – the part that sits in the top of the shaker with holes in it. Straining gets rid of any unwanted bits in your drink as you pour it into the glass. It also stops the ice you shake with from tipping into your glass. Sometimes a cocktail requires 'double straining' – basically, passing it through a strainer twice (or through two strainers put together).

TECHNIQUES & TERMS

Muddling – This technique requires a muddler (see page 13), although the end of a wooden spoon also does the job! Muddling gently 'bruises' a fresh ingredient (for example mint leaves or fruit segments) so that they release their flavours into the drink. Be careful not to 'over muddle' herbs as this can introduce unwanted bitterness.

Shaking – Using a cocktail shaker doesn't simply mix the ingredients, it also chills them. When you've added the ingredients and ice, hold the shaker in both hands – one hand on top and the other on the base – and give it a sharp shake. When waters begin to condense on the outside of the shaker, it means that the cocktail inside is chilled.

Dry shaking – As 'Shaking' above, but you don't put ice in the shaker. This is usually used when a recipe contains egg whites. Dry shaking allow the proteins of the whites to coagulate, aerate and create a foam.

Stirring – The best and most effective way to stir a cocktail is with a bar spoon, or a metal or wooden stick. It's a gentler way to combine ingredients than shaking. Make your stirring slow, steady and smooth. If there's ice in the glass, stirring also helps to melt the ice and slightly dilute the drink.

Simple syrup – For adding sweetness to cocktails. Simply dissolve 300g of caster sugar in 150ml of water in a saucepan over a low heat. Leave to cool and then bottle. Store in the fridge.

'One sip of this will bathe the drooping spirits in delight, beyond the bliss of dreams.'

John Milton

RUM

RUM

CONTENTS

Daquiri

Dark and Stormy

Zombie

Mojito

Piña Colada

Hurricane

Mai Tai

Rum Punch

Caipirinha

Mary Pickford

ABOUT RUM

Rum originated in the Caribbean in the 17th century. In its early days, rum was drunk straight by the poor – it was strong and not particularly pleasant. If you could afford to, you would mix this spirit with sugar and lime ... and that's how rum cocktails started to emerge. However, rum's popularity faded and it wasn't until the 'tiki' movement in the 1930s that it made a comeback. Many tiki cocktails use rum as a base, mixed with fruit juices for a taste of the tropics. Different types of rum have different qualities. The most common types are: dark; white (or light); gold (or amber); and spiced.

THE LITTLE BOOK OF COCKTAILS

DAIQUIRI

DAIQUIRI

SERVES: 1 | SERVED IN: COUPE GLASS

The daiquiri is a classic rum sour drink with its origins in Cuba in the late 1800s. Because rum is made from sugar, it has a natural sweetness that works beautifully with the hit of sour citrus. You'll find lots of variations on the daiquiri recipe, so experiment to find out what proportions of rum and lime work best for your tastebuds.

YOU WILL NEED

45ml light rum

30ml fresh lime juice

1 tsp of simple syrup (see page 17)

Slice of lime, to garnish

METHOD

1. Put ice in a cocktail shaker and pour in all the ingredients.
2. Shake until the shaker is cold to touch.
3. Strain into a chilled glass.
4. Garnish with a slice of lime.

BARTENDER TIP

Create a delicious Strawberry Daiquiri by muddling a handful of fresh strawberries in the cocktail shaker before continuing with step 1 above.

DARK AND STORMY

SERVES: 1 | SERVED IN: HIGHBALL GLASS

The Dark and Stormy originated in Bermuda in the mid-19th century. It's a mixture of sweet, mellow rum, spicy ginger beer and zingy lime. Unstirred, the dark rum floats on top of the ginger beer and looks like a gathering storm cloud.

YOU WILL NEED

120ml ginger beer

60ml dark rum

15ml fresh lime juice

Wedge of lime, to garnish

METHOD

1. Fill the glass with ice. Add the ginger beer and lime juice. Top up with the rum.
2. Garnish with a wedge of lime.
3. Stir before drinking – once you've enjoyed the storm clouds!

BARTENDER TIP

Don't be tempted to use ginger ale in place of ginger beer. Ginger ale is just carbonated water flavoured with ginger, whereas ginger beer is brewed and fermented, which works better with rum.

THE LITTLE BOOK OF COCKTAILS

DARK AND STORMY

THE LITTLE BOOK OF COCKTAILS

ZOMBIE

ZOMBIE

SERVES: 1 | SERVED IN: COLLINS GLASS

Proceed with caution when drinking this cocktail! (The clue is in the name.) The Zombie is a blend of three different rums and packs quite a punch. The anise liqueur and Angostura bitters contribute to its intensity – you won't need more than one!

YOU WILL NEED

- 25ml white rum
- 25ml dark rum
- 1 tbsp overproof rum (see Bartender tip below)
- 25ml fresh lime juice
- 1.25ml Pernod (anise liqueur)
- 100ml pineapple juice
- Dash Angostura bitters
- 1 tsp grenadine
- Sprigs of mint, maraschino cherries and orange slices, to garnish

METHOD

1. Fill a cocktail shaker with ice and add the rums, lime juice, Pernod, pineapple juice and Angostura bitters. Shake well until the outside of the shaker is cold to touch.
2. Strain into a glass filled with ice. Slowly pour over the grenadine.
3. Garnish with the mint, cherries and orange slices.

BARTENDER TIP

Overproof rum is technically any rum which has an alcohol content of over 50% and can be as high as 80%. It is often used as a base for strong tiki cocktails.

MOJITO

SERVES: 1 | SERVED IN: COLLINS OR HIGHBALL GLASS

One of Cuba's oldest cocktails, the name 'mojito' comes from the African word 'mojo', which means to cast a charm or spell. Sweet, citrusy and herby, this is a refreshing summer drink, guaranteed to cool you down on a sultry day or night.

YOU WILL NEED

- 25ml white rum
- 120ml soda water
- 10 fresh mint leaves
- ½ a lime, cut into 4 wedges
- 2 tsp sugar, or to taste

METHOD

1. Put the mint leaves and one of the lime wedges into the glass and muddle to release the oils and juice.
3. Add the sugar and two more lime wedges. Muddle again.
4. Fill the glass with ice (almost to the top but not quite) and then add the rum.
5. Add the soda water and stir.
6. Serve garnished with the last wedge of lime.

BARTENDER TIP

By adding fruits at the muddling stage, you can create your own variation on a mojito. Try adding raspberries, strawberries, or even cucumber.

THE LITTLE BOOK OF COCKTAILS

MOJITO

THE LITTLE BOOK OF COCKTAILS

PIÑA COLADA

PIÑA COLADA

SERVES: 1 | SERVED IN: POCO GRANDE/PIÑA COLADA GLASS

Nothing says 'holiday' quite like a Piña Colada! It's a firm beach bar and poolside favourite, and thankfully, this refreshing, sweet cocktail is super easy to make at home. Now, there's no need to wait until you're on a tropical beach to enjoy it.

YOU WILL NEED

120ml pineapple juice

60ml white rum

60ml coconut cream

Wedge of pineapple, to garnish

METHOD

1. Add ice to a cocktail shaker and pour in the rum and coconut cream.
2. Shake vigorously for 10 to 15 seconds.
3. Strain into the glass filled with a handful of crushed ice. Top up with the pineapple juice. Stir gently.
4. Serve garnished with a wedge of pineapple (and a cocktail umbrella or pineapple leaf!)

BARTENDER TIP

To make crushed ice, place ice cubes in a clean tea towel or sealable bag and gently crush with a blunt kitchen utensil, for example a rolling pin. Do this just before you need the ice as it will melt more quickly than ice cubes.

HURRICANE

SERVES: 1 | SERVED IN: HURRICANE GLASS

The Hurricane was invented in the 1940s in New Orleans. It's fruity, sweet and pretty boozy. The name for the drink comes from the glass it's served in, which resembles a hurricane lamp. This is a tropical cocktail, so enjoy it as you imagine yourself holed up in a bar waiting for a seasonal storm to pass.

YOU WILL NEED

- 60ml white rum
- 60ml dark rum
- 60ml passionfruit juice
- 30ml orange juice
- 15ml grenadine
- 15ml simple syrup (see page 17)
- ½ a lime, juiced
- A slice of orange or lime, and a fresh or maraschino cherry, to garnish

METHOD

1. Fill a cocktail shaker with ice and add all the ingredients. Shake well until the shaker is cold to touch.
2. Strain into a glass filled with crushed ice.
3. Garnish with a slice of orange or lime and a skewered fresh or maraschino cherry.

BARTENDER TIP

Many tiki cocktails, including the Hurricane, are known for their alcoholic strength but mild flavour. You might not appreciate how potent they are, so go easy!

THE LITTLE BOOK OF COCKTAILS

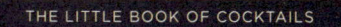

HURRICANE

THE LITTLE BOOK OF COCKTAILS

MAI TAI

MAI TAI

SERVES: 1 | SERVED IN: DOUBLE ROCKS GLASS

The Mai Tai is one of the most famous tiki drinks in the world. It's a tart, strong cocktail that's all about the rum flavour, but with subtle citrus notes. Recommended for people who like strong drinks with just a hint of sweetness.

YOU WILL NEED

45ml white rum

22.5ml orange curaçao

22.5ml fresh lime juice

15ml orgeat syrup (made with almonds, not suitable if you have a nut allergy)

15ml dark rum

Lime slice and sprig of mint, to garnish

METHOD

1. Fill a cocktail shaker with ice and add the white rum, curaçao, lime juice and orgeat syrup. Shake for five seconds.
2. Pour into a double rocks glass over ice.
3. Gently pour in the dark rum so that it 'floats' on the top.
4. Garnish with a slice of lime and a sprig of mint.

BARTENDER TIP

To release the oil in the mint garnish, slap the mint sprig against the back of your palm before adding to your drink.

RUM PUNCH

SERVES: 6 | SERVED IN: HURRICANE GLASS

If you want to savour the essence of the tropics in a glass, rum punch is a guaranteed crowd-pleaser. (Which is why the recipe here is for more than one person!) A punch is a cocktail that consists of spirit, citrus and sugar. Rum works well with most mixers but is especially delicious with fruit juices.

YOU WILL NEED

525ml fresh orange juice

225ml fresh lime juice

450ml golden rum

150ml simple syrup (see page 17)

3 dashes grenadine syrup

3 dashes bitters

2 pinches freshly grated nutmeg

Orange slices and maraschino cherries, to garnish

METHOD

1. Pour the fruit juices, rum, simple syrup, grenadine and bitters into a large jug. Stir well.
2. Leave in the fridge for one hour to chill.
3. Serve with ice and sprinkle over the nutmeg. Garnish with an orange slice and a cherry.

BARTENDER TIP

You can swap the golden rum for equal measures of light and dark rum. This adds a slightly different balance of rum flavours to the punch.

THE LITTLE BOOK OF COCKTAILS

RUM PUNCH

THE LITTLE BOOK OF COCKTAILS

CAIPIRINHA

CAIPIRINHA

SERVES: 1 | SERVED IN: HIGHBALL GLASS

The Caipirinha (kai-puh-ree-nyuh) is the national cocktail of Brazil. Traditionally, it uses cachaça, a type of distilled alcohol made from fermented sugarcane juice, but you can replace that with white rum. Overall, this refreshing cocktail is a lovely blend of sweet, sour and strong flavours.

YOU WILL NEED

½ large lime, cut into wedges

50ml cachaça or white rum

20ml simple syrup (see page 17)

METHOD

1. Using a muddler, squash the lime in a glass to release the juice and oils.
2. Pour in the cachaça or rum and simple syrup.
3. Add ice cubes and stir before serving.

BARTENDER TIP

To make a delicious Caipirinha Maracuja, simply stir in the pulp of three passion fruits after muddling the lime.

MARY PICKFORD

SERVES: 1 | SERVED IN: COUPE GLASS

This is a crisp, balanced cocktail that packs a punch. Mary Pickford was a popular Canadian actress and it's believed this cocktail was created for her during a trip to Cuba in the 1920s. With its classic pineapple and rum combination, it has a definite taste of the tropics.

YOU WILL NEED

45ml white rum

45ml unsweetened pineapple juice

1 tsp maraschino liqueur

¼ tsp grenadine

Maraschino cherry, to garnish

METHOD

1. Fill a cocktail shaker with ice. Add the rum, pineapple juice, liqueur and grenadine. Shake well until the shaker is cold to touch.
2. Strain into the glass.
3. Serve with a skewered cherry.

BARTENDER TIP

Try replacing the pineapple juice with fresh pineapple. Before Step 1, put three pineapple wedges in the cocktail shaker and muddle to release the juices. Then continue with the recipe.

THE LITTLE BOOK OF COCKTAILS

MARY PICKFORD

VODKA

> 'Money, like vodka, turns a person into an eccentric.'
>
> *Anton Chekhov*

VODKA

CONTENTS

Vodka Martini

Espresso Martini

Bloody Mary

White Russian

Vodka Tonic

Moscow Mule

Screwdriver

Sea Breeze

Cosmopolitan

Long Island Iced Tea

ABOUT VODKA

Vodka is a clear distilled spirit made from grains or potatoes, known for its smooth, neutral flavour. Vodka originates from Eastern Europe – both Russia and Poland lay claim to inventing it – and the word 'vodka' derives from the Slavic word 'voda', which means water. It was first made in the 8th or 9th century and was initially used for medicinal purposes. By the 14th century, it had become popular as a drink but it wasn't until the 18th century that it started to look like the vodka we know today. Vodka's versatility makes it a popular base for countless cocktails and it's a staple in both home bars and upmarket cocktail lounges.

VODKA MARTINI

SERVES: 1 | SERVED IN: MARTINI GLASS

This is a sleek and sophisticated cocktail, popularised by James Bond's preference for a vodka martini 'shaken, not stirred' and represents the timeless refinement of cocktail culture. This is the stirred version of the recipe. Who wants to be James Bond anyway?!

YOU WILL NEED

75ml vodka

15ml dry vermouth

Green olive and/or lemon twist, for garnish

METHOD

1. Pour the vodka and dry vermouth into a cocktail shaker with ice. Stir well, don't shake – treating it gently will prevent it from clouding.

2. Strain into a chilled martini glass.

3. Garnish with a lemon twist or push your olive onto a cocktail stick and float it in the glass.

BARTENDER TIP

To make a lemon twist garnish, simply cut a round slice from the thickest part of the lemon and make one cut from the edge to the middle. Remove the flesh and pith from the peel. Twist the peel into a 'spring' shape.

THE LITTLE BOOK OF COCKTAILS

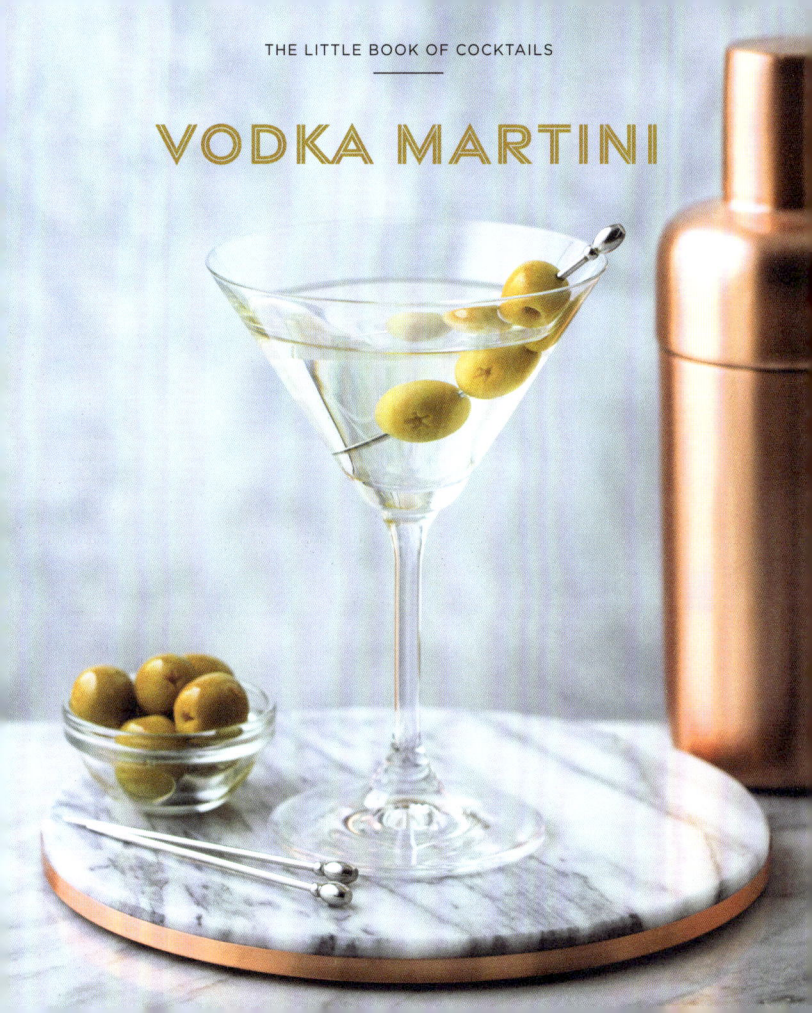

VODKA MARTINI

THE LITTLE BOOK OF COCKTAILS

ESPRESSO MARTINI

ESPRESSO MARTINI

SERVES: 1 | SERVED IN: MARTINI GLASS

The espresso martini is a lively mix of vodka, espresso and Kahlúa. It provides a bold caffeine boost with smooth, rich flavours. Garnished with coffee beans, it's a perfect choice for an elegant after-dinner or late-night drink.

YOU WILL NEED

45ml vodka	15ml simple syrup (see page 17)
45ml Kahlúa	Coffee beans, to garnish
30ml espresso	

METHOD

1. Make an espresso and leave to cool completely.
2. Add the vodka, Kahlúa, espresso, simple syrup and a handful of ice cubes to a cocktail shaker.
3. Shake vigorously for 30 seconds.
4. Strain into a chilled glass quickly – do it quickly to create the foam.
5. Serve garnished with coffee beans.

BARTENDER TIP

Make sure the espresso is completely cold before you use it. If it's still warm, the ice will melt and you'll end up with a watery cocktail that doesn't have quite the same impact!

BLOODY MARY

SERVES: 1 | SERVED IN: COLLINS GLASS

The Bloody Mary is a savoury cocktail featuring vodka, tomato juice and an array of spices. It's a brunch favourite and is favoured for its potential hangover-relief properties! Like many classic cocktails, recipes vary widely, so don't be afraid to experiment to find the flavour that suits you.

YOU WILL NEED

Celery salt

1 lemon wedge

1 lime wedge

60ml vodka

120ml tomato juice

2 tsp horseradish sauce

2 dashes Tabasco sauce

2 dashes Worcestershire sauce

1 pinch ground black pepper

1 pinch smoked paprika

Sprig of basil, green olives, lime wedge and celery stalk, to garnish

METHOD

1. Put some celery salt onto a plate. Rub a wedge of lemon around the rim of a class and then roll the glass in the celery salt until the rim is coated. Add a handful of ice and set aside.

2. Squeeze the lemon and lime wedges into a cocktail shaker and then drop in. Add the vodka, tomato juice, horseradish, Tabasco and Worcestershire sauces, pepper and paprika, plus a pinch of celery salt. Shake gently.

3. Strain into the glass. Garnish with the basil, olives, lime and celery stalk.

THE LITTLE BOOK OF COCKTAILS

BLOODY MARY

THE LITTLE BOOK OF COCKTAILS

WHITE RUSSIAN

WHITE RUSSIAN

SERVES: 1 | SERVED IN: OLD FASHIONED GLASS

The ingredients in a White Russian blend together to create a smooth and decadent cocktail. It's deliciously rich and creamy, and thoroughly indulgent. It became a film-fan favourite thanks to the cult movie *The Big Lebowski* (1998) where the main character drank it throughout.

YOU WILL NEED

60ml vodka

30ml Kahlúa

30ml double cream

METHOD

1. Fill a cocktail shaker with ice and pour in the vodka, Kahlúa and double cream. Shake vigorously until the shaker is cold to touch.
2. Strain into a glass.
3. Serve over ice ('on the rocks').

BARTENDER TIP

Try replacing the cream with almond milk to make it slightly less heavy. You can also replace the Kahlúa with amaretto. NB: neither of these substitutes are suitable for anyone with a nut allergy.

VODKA TONIC

SERVES: 1 | SERVED IN: HIGHBALL GLASS

Why do you need a recipe for Vodka Tonic? It's simple, isn't it? Yes, but, like with a G&T, it pays to get the balance right to enjoy the flavours at their best. This refreshing and simple drink allows the smoothness of the vodka to shine, making it a timeless choice for any occasion.

YOU WILL NEED

150ml tonic water

50ml vodka

Lime wedges and mint leaves, to garnish

METHOD

1. Fill a glass with ice.
2. Pour in the vodka.
3. Slowly pour in the tonic water. Stir gently.
4. Garnish with lime wedges and mint leaves.

BARTENDER TIP

Pouring in the tonic water too quickly causes it to fizz up at the top of the drink, releasing lots of carbon dioxide. The slower you pour, the more fizz you'll keep in your drink!

THE LITTLE BOOK OF COCKTAILS

VODKA TONIC

THE LITTLE BOOK OF COCKTAILS

MOSCOW MULE

MOSCOW MULE

SERVES: 1 | SERVED IN: COPPER MUG

The Moscow Mule is a refreshing cocktail made with vodka, zingy lime juice and a spicy kick of ginger beer. It's traditionally served in a copper mug, which, as well as looking good, keeps the cocktail icy cold. Copper also interacts with the ingredients, boosting the flavours of the ginger beer and lime.

YOU WILL NEED

60ml vodka

15ml fresh lime juice

120ml ginger beer

Wedge of lime and sprig of mint, to garnish

METHOD

1. Fill the mug to three-quarters full of crushed ice. Pour in the vodka and lime juice.
2. Top with the ginger beer and stir gently.
3. Serve garnished with a sprig of mint and a lime wedge.

BARTENDER TIP

To make a Mexican Mule, replace the vodka with the same quantity of tequila. Use whiskey instead of vodka to make an Irish Mule.

SCREWDRIVER

SERVES: 1 | SERVED IN: COLLINS OR HIGHBALL GLASS

The Screwdriver cocktail is a simple yet stylish mix of vodka and orange juice, with a distinctively vibrant, citrusy flavour. The unusual name comes from the story that American oil workers in the 1940s used screwdrivers as a utensil to stir their vodka and orange as there was nothing more suitable to hand.

YOU WILL NEED

25ml vodka

125ml orange juice

Slice of orange, to garnish

METHOD

1. Fill a glass with ice.
2. Add the vodka to the glass and then top up with orange juice. Stir gently.
3. Garnish with a slice of orange.

BARTENDER TIP

To turn a Screwdriver into a Harvey Wallbanger, slowly pour 10ml of Galliano (a liqueur made with vanilla, herbs and spices) on top of the drink so that it 'floats'.

THE LITTLE BOOK OF COCKTAILS

SCREWDRIVER

THE LITTLE BOOK OF COCKTAILS

SEA BREEZE

SEA BREEZE

SERVES: 1 | SERVED IN: HIGHBALL GLASS

The Sea Breeze is a simple summer classic. It's a crisp blend of vodka, cranberry juice and grapefruit juice and full of tangy flavours. Make it your first choice for a summer evening to evoke a coastal vibe!

YOU WILL NEED

50ml vodka

135ml cranberry juice

15ml pink grapefruit juice

Wedge of lime, to garnish

METHOD

1. Measure the vodka, cranberry juice and grapefruit juice into a glass.
2. Add a handful of ice. Stir slowly to combine the ingredients.
3. Serve garnished with a lime wedge.

BARTENDER TIP

Don't like grapefruit juice? You can create a Bay Breeze by swapping the grapefruit juice for pineapple juice.

COSMOPOLITAN

SERVES: 1 | SERVED IN: COUPE GLASS

The Cosmo is a fun and fruity cocktail. It has been well-known since its creation in the 1980s, but it became hugely popular in the 1990s thanks to the TV show, *Sex and the City*. For a longer version, serve this drink in a highball glass with extra cranberry juice, but be aware that this will alter the overall balance of this classic recipe.

YOU WILL NEED

45ml vodka

22.5ml Cointreau

22.5ml fresh lime juice

15ml cranberry juice

Wedge of lime, to garnish

METHOD

1. Fill a cocktail shaker with ice. Pour in the vodka, Cointreau, lime juice and cranberry juice and shake until the shaker is cold to touch.
2. Strain into a chilled glass.
3. Garnish with a wedge of lime before serving.

BARTENDER TIP

To chill glasses, place them in the coldest place in your fridge (this is normally the top shelf at the back). Leave for at least one hour, or up to four hours.

THE LITTLE BOOK OF COCKTAILS

COSMOPOLITAN

THE LITTLE BOOK OF COCKTAILS

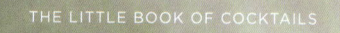

LONG ISLAND ICED TEA

LONG ISLAND ICED TEA

SERVES: 1 | SERVED IN: COLLINS GLASS

This isn't strictly a 'vodka' cocktail as it also contains equal measures of rum, tequila and gin. It packs a potent alcoholic punch thanks to all the boozy ingredients. Finally, there's no tea in this drink – the name comes from it being tea-coloured! So, don't add milk …

YOU WILL NEED

- 22.5ml vodka
- 22.5ml white rum
- 22.5ml tequila
- 22.5ml gin
- 22.5ml triple sec
- 22.5ml simple syrup (see page 17)
- 22.5ml fresh lemon juice
- Cola, to top up
- Lemon wedge, to garnish

METHOD

1. Add all ingredients apart from the cola to a jug. Half fill the jug with ice and stir until the outside feels cold.
2. Top with the cola and stir again.
3. Strain the iced drink into a glass filled with ice.
4. Garnish with a lemon wedge and serve with a straw.

BARTENDER TIP

Triple sec is an orange-flavoured liqueur that originally came from France. If you don't have any to hand, Grand Marnier, Cointreau or even orange juice are good alternatives.

GIN

'Most cocktails today are made with gin and ingenuity.'

Irma S. Rombauer

GIN

CONTENTS

French 75

Classic G&T

Aviation

Clover Club

Gimlet

Gin Basil Smash

The Last Word

Negroni

Old Friend

Ramos Gin Fizz

ABOUT GIN

Gin originated as a medicinal liquor made by monks across Europe. Modern gin, as we know it, arrived from Belgium and the Netherlands in the form of jenever (or 'Dutch gin') and became hugely popular in England. Gin's distinctive flavour comes from juniper berries with their fruity citrus flavour and aromatic, piney spiciness. Different gins include a range of 'botanicals' (fruits, herbs, spices) that give them their distinct flavour in addition to the juniper berries. By the second half of the 19th century, gin became popular as a cocktail ingredient, reaching the height of fashion in the 1920s. There are more classic cocktails made with gin than any other spirit.

FRENCH 75

SERVES: 1 | SERVED IN: CHAMPAGNE FLUTE

The French 75 is a sophisticated and elegant cocktail. The tartness of the citrus balances beautifully with the bubbles in the champagne and its effervescence makes this a perfect drink for celebrations. The name comes from comparing the kick of the cocktail to a 75mm Howitzer gun!

YOU WILL NEED

45ml gin

15ml lemon juice

7.5ml simple syrup (see page 17)

Champagne, chilled

Lemon peel, to garnish

METHOD

1. Fill a cocktail shaker with ice. Pour in the gin, lemon juice and simple syrup. Shake well to combine. The shaker should feel cold to touch.
2. Strain into a glass and top up with the champagne.
3. Garnish with a piece of lemon peel.

BARTENDER TIP

The trick to making a fantastic French 75 is to ensure the gin and champagne are both well chilled before mixing.

THE LITTLE BOOK OF COCKTAILS

FRENCH 75

THE LITTLE BOOK OF COCKTAILS

CLASSIC G&T

CLASSIC G&T

SERVES: 1 | SERVED IN: HIGHBALL GLASS

The classic G&T might be simple, but it is packed full of flavour and epitomises timeless elegance. Its simplicity allows the gin's botanical notes to really shine through. Experiment with different brands of gin and it will be a new experience every time.

YOU WILL NEED

50ml gin

Tonic water (chilled)

Wedge of lime

METHOD

1. Fill a chilled highball glass with ice cubes.
2. Pour the gin over the ice. Top up with the tonic water, making sure to pour slowly.
3. Gently squeeze a wedge of lime into the glass and then drop it in. Stir gently.

BARTENDER TIP

To help keep lots of bubbles in the tonic, gently pour the tonic water down a spoon to maintain carbonation.

AVIATION

SERVES: 1 | SERVED IN: COUPE GLASS

The name for this cocktail comes from the world's obsession in the early 1900s with anything aeronautical. It's a classic aperitif, so is guaranteed not to spoil your appetite. The elegant Aviation has a unique floral and sharp flavour, and, with its violet hue, you'll take to the skies!

YOU WILL NEED

60ml gin

7.5ml Crème de Violette or Creme Yvette

15ml maraschino liqueur

22.5ml fresh lemon juice

Maraschino cherry, to garnish

METHOD

1. Add the ingredients into the cocktail shaker filled with ice. Shake well to mix thoroughly and until the shaker is cold to touch.
2. Strain into the glass.
3. To garnish, drop in the cherry.

BARTENDER TIP

Don't skimp on the shaking. The Aviation cocktail needs to be shaken vigorously to ensure a frothy texture.

THE LITTLE BOOK OF COCKTAILS

AVIATION

THE LITTLE BOOK OF COCKTAILS

CLOVER CLUB

CLOVER CLUB

SERVES: 1 | SERVED IN: COUPE GLASS

The Clover Club is a pre-Prohibition classic. It takes its name from a men's social club that met at the Philadelphia hotel where the cocktail was first made. This elegant cocktail is a delightful balance of tart and sweet flavours and has a smooth, creamy texture.

YOU WILL NEED

60ml gin

22.5ml fresh lemon juice

22.5ml raspberry syrup

1 egg white

Raspberries, to garnish

METHOD

1. Dry shake (without ice) the egg white in an empty cocktail shaker for 15 seconds.
2. Add the remaining ingredients and shake again.
3. Strain into a chilled glass.
4. Garnish with raspberries skewered on a cocktail stick.

BARTENDER TIP

If you fancy a variation on the Clover Club or don't like gin, you can use vodka instead. It adds a spicier taste and more depth of flavour.

GIMLET

SERVES: 1 | SERVED IN: COUPE OR MARTINI GLASS

With its crisp flavour, the Gimlet is a big favourite of gin enthusiasts and promises to wake up your tastebuds. It originated in the 19th century when the Royal Navy mixed gin with lime cordial to prevent scurvy.

YOU WILL NEED

50ml gin

50ml Rose's lime cordial

Slice of lime, to garnish

METHOD

1. Put the ingredients in a cocktail shaker filled with ice. Shake until the shaker is cold to touch.
2. Strain into a chilled glass filled with fresh ice.
3. Garnish with a slice of lime.

BARTENDER TIP

Use a highball glass for your Gimlet, top up with soda water and you'll have a Gin Rickey.

THE LITTLE BOOK OF COCKTAILS

GIMLET

THE LITTLE BOOK OF COCKTAILS

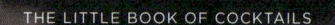

GIN BASIL SMASH

GIN BASIL SMASH

SERVES: 1 | SERVED IN: ROCKS OR OLD FASHIONED GLASS

This refreshing, herby cocktail combines sweet, sour and bitter notes. The tang of the lemon finishes off the taste experience. This is a great cocktail to enjoy in the summer. If you want to reduce the basil flavour, don't muddle the leaves.

YOU WILL NEED

50ml gin

25ml fresh lemon juice

15ml simple syrup (see page 17)

1 bunch of basil leaves, 3-4 reserved to garnish

METHOD

1. Put the basil and lemon into a cocktail shaker. Gently muddle the lemon and basil to crush them and release the flavours.
2. Add the simple syrup and gin and then top up the shaker with ice. Shake vigorously until the shaker feels cold to touch.
3. Double strain into an ice-filled rocks or Old Fashioned glass.
4. Garnish with the reserved basil leaves to serve.

BARTENDER TIP

Try not to muddle ingredients to oblivion! Add the ingredients that are harder to muddle first (e.g. lime wedges and sugar). More delicate ingredients such as herbs, that require less muddling, can be added afterwards.

THE LAST WORD

SERVES: 1 | SERVED IN: COUPE OR MARTINI GLASS

The Last Word cocktail is a balanced mix of gin, green Chartreuse, maraschino liqueur, and fresh lime juice. Together, these create a herbal and slightly zesty flavour. It has been described as key lime pie in a glass!

YOU WILL NEED

22.5ml gin

22.5ml freshly squeezed lime juice

22.5ml maraschino liqueur

22.5ml green Chartreuse

Lime wedge and cherry, to garnish

METHOD

1. Fill a cocktail shaker with ice and add all the ingredients. Shake vigorously for 15 seconds.
2. Strain into a chilled glass.
3. Serve garnished with a wedge of lime and a cherry on a skewer.

BARTENDER TIP

Chartreuse is a French liqueur made with 130 herbs and botanicals. Green Chartreuse has flavours of lime, citrus spice and freshly cut herbs. If drinking it neat, always serve VERY chilled.

THE LITTLE BOOK OF COCKTAILS

THE LAST WORD

THE LITTLE BOOK OF COCKTAILS

NEGRONI

NEGRONI

SERVES: 1 | SERVED IN: LOWBALL GLASS

The Negroni is a bold cocktail known for its rich, complex flavours. It's a bitter drink but the vermouth and orange garnish provide a sweet fruitiness to balance it out. This Italian classic has become a much-loved aperitif.

YOU WILL NEED

30ml gin

30ml Campari

30ml sweet vermouth

1 wedge of orange

METHOD

1. Fill a cocktail shaker with ice and add the gin, Campari and vermouth.
2. Shake to mix completely. Strain into the glass.
3. Add ice and an orange wedge.

BARTENDER TIP

There are lots of Negroni variations. Use Aperol instead of Campari and dry vermouth instead of sweet vermouth to create a Contessa.

OLD FRIEND

SERVES: 1 | SERVED IN: COUPE GLASS

The Old Friend is a sophisticated combination of flavours, combining bitter and sweet tones. The floral sweetness of the elderflower liqueur works well with the gin and the Aperol brings a bitter edge. Add the refreshing citrus of grapefruit juice to complete this invigorating drink.

YOU WILL NEED

30ml gin

15ml Aperol

10ml elderflower liqueur

22.5ml grapefruit juice

Grapefruit or lemon twist, to garnish

METHOD

1. Fill a cocktail shaker with ice. Pour in all the ingredients. Shake for 10–15 seconds until the outside of the shaker is chilled.
2. Strain into a chilled glass.
3. Garnish with a grapefruit or lemon twist on the side of the glass.

BARTENDER TIP

For a non-alcoholic alternative, replace the elderflower liqueur with a small amount of elderflower syrup or diluted cordial.

THE LITTLE BOOK OF COCKTAILS

OLD FRIEND

RAMOS GIN FIZZ

RAMOS GIN FIZZ

SERVES: 1 | SERVED IN: HIGHBALL GLASS

The Ramos Gin Fizz is a classic New Orleans cocktail. It needs to be shaken vigorously to achieve its signature froth and creamy consistency, so be prepared for an arm workout! A refreshing and indulgent treat, the orange flower water provides delicate, floral tones.

YOU WILL NEED

- 50ml gin
- 15ml fresh lemon juice
- 15ml fresh lime juice
- 30ml simple syrup (see page 17)
- Dash of orange flower water
- 1 egg white
- 60ml cream
- Soda water

METHOD

1. Add all the ingredients (apart from the soda water) to a cocktail shaker. Dry shake (without ice) for at least two minutes to froth up the egg white.
2. Add a handful of ice to the cocktail shaker. Shake until the shaker is ice cold to touch.
3. Strain into a highball glass, over ice.
4. Top up the glass with the soda water.

BARTENDER TIP

As an alternative to egg white, use aquafaba, which is a vegan product. It creates the same froth and silkiness as egg white.

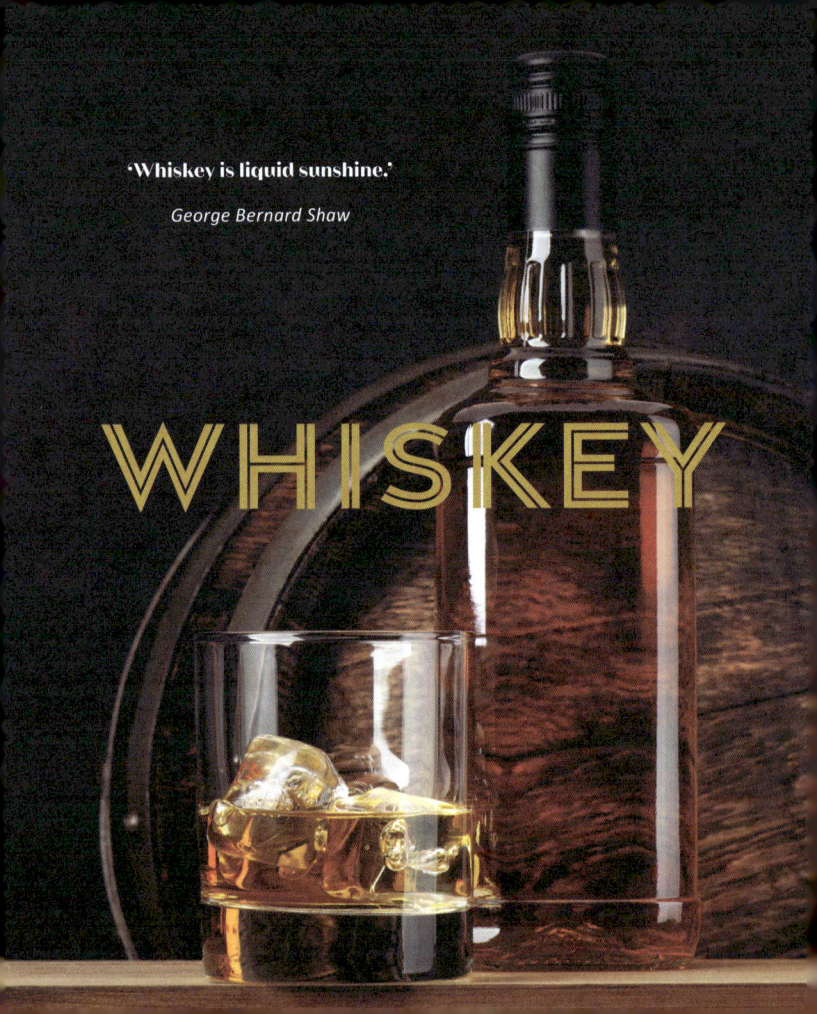

'Whiskey is liquid sunshine.'

George Bernard Shaw

WHISKEY

WHISKEY

CONTENTS

Manhattan

Rusty Nail

Bourbon Sour

Whiskey Highball

Mint Julep

Old Fashioned

Sazerac

John Collins

Hot Toddy

Boulevardier

ABOUT WHISKEY

Whiskey is a distilled spirit made from fermented grain mash, including barley, corn, rye and wheat. The production process involves mashing, fermenting, distilling and aging the spirit in wooden barrels. Originating in Ireland and Scotland, whiskey has evolved into various styles, such as Scotch, Bourbon, Rye and Irish whiskey, each with their own characteristics. Whiskey has long been a favourite ingredient in cocktails, from the simple whiskey and soda to more elaborate concoctions. In fact, it's likely that you've tried a whiskey cocktail at some point, even if you would turn your nose up at whiskey served neat.

MANHATTAN

SERVES: 1 | SERVED IN: COUPE GLASS

The Manhattan, created in the late 1800s, is probably one of the most well-known cocktails of all. This elegant drink is a perfect balance of sweetness, bitterness and whiskey's robust flavour, making it a classic in cocktail culture.

YOU WILL NEED

90ml bourbon

45ml sweet vermouth

2 dashes Angostura bitters

Maraschino cherry, to garnish

METHOD

1. In a mixing glass, combine the bourbon, vermouth and bitters.
2. Add ice and stir until chilled.
3. Strain into a chilled glass.
4. Serve garnished with a skewered maraschino cherry.

BARTENDER TIP

How long you stir a cocktail for depends on the ice you use. Harder, drier ice means you need to stir for longer, around 30 seconds. For softer, smaller cubes, 15 seconds is enough.

THE LITTLE BOOK OF COCKTAILS

MANHATTAN

THE LITTLE BOOK OF COCKTAILS

RUSTY NAIL

RUSTY NAIL

SERVES: 1 | SERVED IN: OLD FASHIONED GLASS

The Rusty Nail is a relative latecomer to the cocktail world, first appearing in its current form in around 1937. The honey and heather hints of Drambuie are a gentle antidote to the harsher Scotch, so this one works especially well for drinkers who are new to whiskey.

YOU WILL NEED

60ml blended Scotch whisky

15ml Drambuie

Lemon twist, to garnish

METHOD

1. Pour the whiskey and Drambuie into the glass.
2. Add lots of ice.
3. Stir gently to combine.
4. Serve garnished with a lemon twist.

BARTENDER TIP

Experiment to find the proportions of whisky and Drambuie that work for you. Less whisky and more Drambuie gives the drink a softer, sweeter edge.

BOURBON SOUR

SERVES: 1 | SERVED IN: OLD FASHIONED OR ROCKS GLASS

A 'sour' can be made with different types of whiskey, but using bourbon (an American whiskey made primarily from corn) makes for a tastebud-pleasing flavour. This a refreshing cocktail that offers a perfect balance of sweet, sour and rich bourbon notes.

YOU WILL NEED

60ml bourbon

22.5ml fresh lemon juice

22.5ml simple syrup (see page 17)

Orange slice and maraschino cherry, to garnish

METHOD

1. Fill a cocktail shaker with ice. Pour in the bourbon, lemon juice and simple syrup.
2. Shake vigorously until the outside of the shaker is very cold.
3. Strain into a glass filled with ice.
4. Garnish with an orange slice and a skewered maraschino cherry.

BARTENDER TIP

The standard formula for a 'sour' drink is two parts spirit, one part sweet and one part sour.

THE LITTLE BOOK OF COCKTAILS

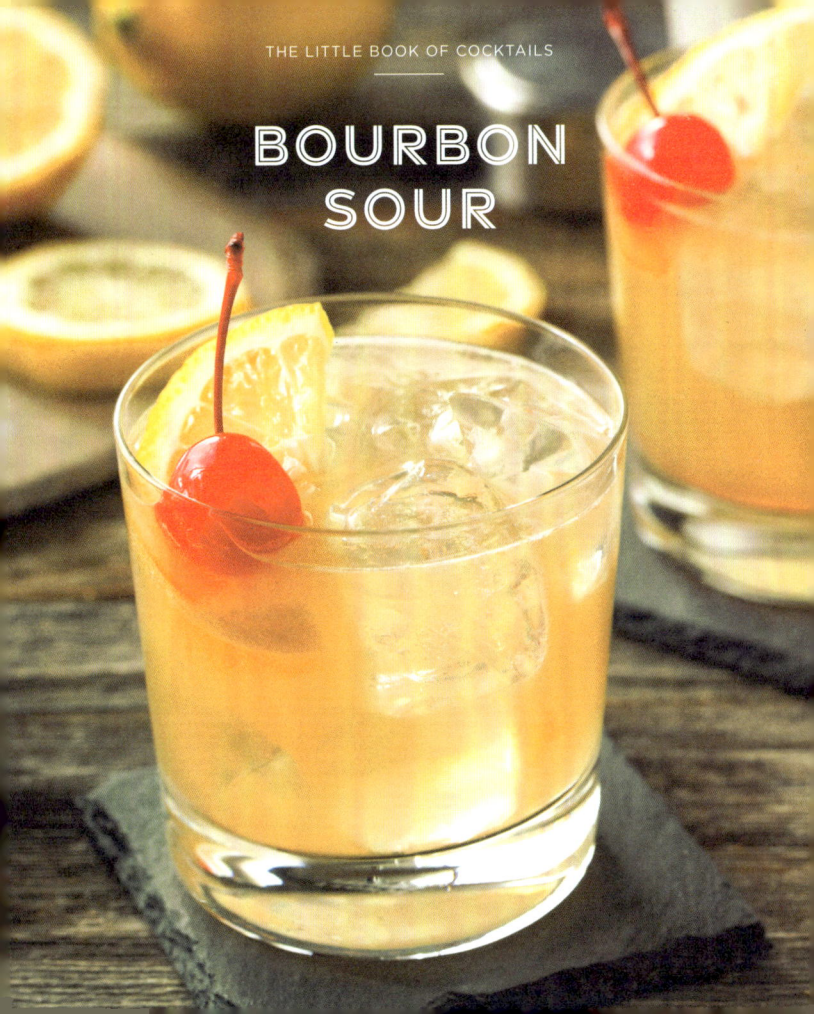

BOURBON SOUR

THE LITTLE BOOK OF COCKTAILS

WHISKEY HIGHBALL

WHISKEY HIGHBALL

SERVES: 1 | SERVED IN: HIGHBALL GLASS

If you're not a huge whiskey drinker, this cocktail is a good introduction and proves that whiskey isn't just for drinking in a pub after a winter walk across the Highlands! A Highball makes for a surprisingly refreshing drink which is great for cooling down on a summer's day.

YOU WILL NEED

50ml whiskey

100–150ml sparkling water

Strip of lemon peel

2–3 mint leaves

METHOD

1. Fill the glass with ice. Add the whisky and then pour in the sparkling water.
2. Add the lemon peel and mint leaves.
3. Stir gently to combine.

BARTENDER TIP

Add a drop or two of Angostura bitters to enhance the flavour of this cocktail. Angostura bitters are spicy, with notes of cloves and cinnamon.

MINT JULEP

SERVES: 1 | SERVED IN: HIGHBALL OR JULEP CUP

This refreshing, minty cocktail is a classic Southern US drink. It is also the signature drink of the Kentucky Derby – an annual horse race that has been run since 1875 – where it is served in an ice-frosted silver julep cup.

YOU WILL NEED

60ml bourbon

7.5ml simple syrup (see page 17)

8 mint leaves

Sprig of mint, to garnish

METHOD

1. In the cup, gently muddle the mint leaves with the syrup to release their flavour.
2. Pour in the bourbon. Fill the cup with crushed ice.
3. Stir until the cup is chilled and frosted on the outside.
4. Add more crushed ice to form a mound of ice at the top of the glass. Top with the sprig of mint and serve.

BARTENDER TIP

Everything about the Mint Julep is intended to be light and refreshing – therefore don't be heavy-handed with the bourbon!

THE LITTLE BOOK OF COCKTAILS

MINT JULEP

THE LITTLE BOOK OF COCKTAILS

OLD FASHIONED

OLD FASHIONED

SERVES: 1 | SERVED IN: OLD FASHIONED OR LOWBALL GLASS

The Old Fashioned is a revered classic that dates back to the early 19th century. It balances the sweetness of sugar with the robust flavour of whiskey. This cocktail epitomises simplicity and elegance and has long been a firm favourite of whiskey fans.

YOU WILL NEED

50ml whiskey or bourbon

1 cube or tsp of brown sugar

2–3 dashes Angostura bitters

Orange peel, to garnish

METHOD

1. Add the sugar and the bitters to a chilled glass. Gently muddle the ingredients together until they're well mixed.
2. Add a dash of the whiskey and some ice cubes. Stir for 20 seconds.
3. Gradually add a little more whiskey and ice, stirring each time and tasting until you find the strength you enjoy.
4. Garnish with a twist of orange peel and serve.

BARTENDER TIP

The purpose of the sugar is to reduce the heat of the alcohol in the whiskey, not to add sweetness. Don't add more sugar than is necessary to balance it out.

SAZERAC

SERVES: 1 | SERVED IN: OLD FASHIONED GLASS

It is thought that the Sazerac is the oldest American cocktail, originating from New Orleans before the American Civil War. It was originally made with cognac but this was replaced by rye whiskey. The result is a bold and aromatic drink with lots of flavour.

YOU WILL NEED

60ml rye whiskey

1 tsp absinthe

1 tsp simple syrup (see page 17)

2–3 dashes Peychaud's Bitters

Lemon peel, to garnish

METHOD

1. Pour the absinthe into the chilled old fashioned glass and swirl until it coats the inside of the glass.
2. Pour the whiskey, simple syrup and bitters over ice in a mixing glass. Stir gently to combine.
3. Strain the mixture into the chilled glass coated with absinthe.
4. Twist the lemon peel over the drink and then use it as a garnish.

BARTENDER TIP

If you don't have any absinthe, you can rinse your glass with Pernod, pastis or another anise-flavoured spirit.

THE LITTLE BOOK OF COCKTAILS

SAZERAC

THE LITTLE BOOK OF COCKTAILS

JOHN COLLINS

JOHN COLLINS

SERVES: 1 | SERVED IN: COLLINS GLASS

The John Collins is an easy to drink cocktail with an effervescent character that makes it perfect for sipping in the summer months. Its simplicity lets the flavour of the whiskey shine through, all nicely balanced with the lemon and syrup.

YOU WILL NEED

45ml bourbon whiskey

30ml fresh lemon juice

15ml simple syrup (see page 17)

60ml soda water

1 orange slice or lemon slice and a maraschino cherry, for garnish

METHOD

1. Fill a glass with ice cubes.
2. Pour in the bourbon, lemon juice and simple syrup. Stir well.
3. Top up the glass with soda water.
4. Garnish with a slice of orange or lemon and a cherry.

BARTENDER TIP

Turn your John Collins into a Tom Collins by replacing the whiskey with 60ml of gin, lowering the amount of lemon juice to 15ml and ditching the cherry.

HOT TODDY

SERVES: 1 | SERVED IN: HEATPROOF GLASS OR MUG

This Hot Toddy is a comforting, warm cocktail perfect for enjoying during the colder months. Known to help relieve cold symptoms, it combines the warming properties of whiskey with the soothing effects of honey and lemon, creating a deliciously restorative hug in a glass.

YOU WILL NEED

25ml whiskey

1½ tsp honey

½ cinnamon stick

200ml boiling water

Juice of ¼ of a lemon

¼ of a sliced lemon and a star anise to garnish

METHOD

1. Whisk together the whisky and the honey in the glass.
2. Add the half cinnamon stick to the glass and top up with the boiling water.
3. Add enough lemon juice to suit your preferred taste. Stir.
4. Garnish with the slice of lemon and star anise. Serve Immediately.

BARTENDER TIP

You don't have to stick with the suggested spices. Try your own combinations. Fresh ginger makes an ideal addition if you're treating cold symptoms.

THE LITTLE BOOK OF COCKTAILS

HOT TODDY

THE LITTLE BOOK OF COCKTAILS

BOULEVARDIER

BOULEVARDIER

SERVES: 1 | SERVED IN: ROCKS GLASS

The Boulevardier is a sophisticated cocktail, blending whiskey, sweet vermouth and Campari. Its rich, bittersweet flavours come from the herbal notes in the Campari and the smooth warmth of the whiskey. This is guaranteed to become a firm favourite in your cocktail repertoire.

YOU WILL NEED

60ml rye whiskey or bourbon

30ml sweet vermouth

30ml Campari

Orange peel, for garnish

METHOD

1. Place all ingredients in a mixing glass. Add ice and stir for 30 seconds.
2. Allow to sit for 30 seconds, then strain into a glass with ice.
3. Garnish with orange peel and serve.

BARTENDER TIP

Stirring a cocktail allows the ice to melt slightly. It also softens the kick of the alcohol without making the drink cloudy (unlike when you shake it).

BRANDY

'The most sensible thing to do to people you hate is to drink their brandy.'

Elizabeth Taylor

BRANDY

CONTENTS

Sidecar

Brandy Alexander

Corpse Reviver No.1

Pisco Sour

Appletini

Metropolitan

Stinger

Depth Bomb

Black Jack

Dulce de Tequila

ABOUT BRANDY

Like many spirits, brandy has been around for centuries. The name 'brandy' comes from the Dutch word *brandewijn*, meaning 'burnt wine', and referring to the way heat is applied to the drink during the distillation process. Brandy is typically aged in wooden casks, which provides the rich, complex flavours and amber colour. It is valued for its warm, smooth profile and versatility. Varieties of brandy include Cognac and Armagnac from France. During the 19th century, it became 'acceptable' to mix brandy with other drinks – and the first brandy cocktails started to emerge.

SIDECAR

SERVES: 1 | SERVED IN: COUPE GLASS

This is an elegant drink with a perfect balance of sweet, tart and smooth flavours. The Sidecar - named after a motorcycle sidecar - is renowned for its simplicity and timeless appeal.

YOU WILL NEED

50ml cognac brandy

25ml Cointreau

25ml fresh lemon juice

1 tsp simple syrup (see page 17)

Orange peel, to garnish

METHOD

1. Put a handful of ice in a cocktail shaker. Add all the ingredients. Shake vigorously until the ingredients are thoroughly combined and until the shaker is icy cold to touch.
2. Strain into a glass.
3. Garnish with a twist of orange peel.

BARTENDER TIP

As this is a sour cocktail, you might choose to add a sugar rim to the glass.

THE LITTLE BOOK OF COCKTAILS

SIDECAR

THE LITTLE BOOK OF COCKTAILS

BRANDY ALEXANDER

BRANDY ALEXANDER

SERVES: 1 | SERVED IN: COUPE GLASS

The Brandy Alexander is a rich and creamy cocktail that's typically garnished with a sprinkle of nutmeg. It's an indulgent drink, known for its smooth, chocolatey flavour, which makes it a fantastic dessert or after dinner cocktail. Brandy is also believed to settle the stomach after a big meal.

YOU WILL NEED

22.5ml brandy

22.5ml double cream

22.5ml dark crème de cacao

Pinch of ground nutmeg

METHOD

1. Place all the liquid ingredients in a mixing glass.
2. Stir well to combine.
3. Pour the mixture into a chilled glass.
4. Serve garnished with a sprinkle of nutmeg.

BARTENDER TIP

Make this even more of a dessert cocktail and serve with sponge fingers for dipping!

CORPSE REVIVER NO. 1

SERVES: 1 | SERVED IN: MARTINI GLASS

As the name suggests, this cocktail was created to relieve hangovers. It combines the warmth of brandy, the fruitiness of Calvados (apple brandy) and the herbal notes of sweet vermouth to create a rich, complex flavour. Perfect if you need a pick-me-up on the morning after the night before.

YOU WILL NEED

60ml Cognac brandy

30ml Calvados brandy

30ml sweet vermouth

Lemon twist, to garnish

METHOD

1. Pour all the liquid ingredients into a mixing glass with ice.
2. Stir well to combine and until chilled.
3. Strain into a chilled glass.
4. Serve garnished with a twist of lemon.

BARTENDER TIP

Try rounding out the flavour of this cocktail even more by adding a few dashes of orange bitters.

THE LITTLE BOOK OF COCKTAILS

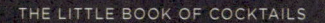

CORPSE REVIVER NO. 1

THE LITTLE BOOK OF COCKTAILS

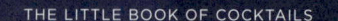

PISCO SOUR

PISCO SOUR

SERVES: 1 | SERVED IN: COUPE OR OLD FASHIONED GLASS

The Pisco Sour is a vibrant, tangy cocktail originating from Peru. Made with pisco (a type of brandy), this refreshing drink balances sweet and sour flavours. It is celebrated for its smooth, refreshing profile. If you don't have pisco, use grappa, white rum or tequila instead.

YOU WILL NEED

60ml pisco

30ml fresh lime juice

22.5ml simple syrup (see page 17)

1 fresh egg white

1 dash Angostura bitters

METHOD

1. Put the pisco, lime, simple syrup and egg white in a cocktail shaker, without any ice. Dry shake vigorously until the egg white is foamy.
2. Add ice to shaker and shake again until well chilled.
3. Strain into a chilled glass.
4. Dash the bitters on top of the egg foam to garnish.

BARTENDER TIP

Freshly squeezed lime (and lemon) juice will last for up to 24 hours at room temperature, or 3-4 days in the fridge.

APPLETINI

SERVES: 1 | SERVED IN: MARTINI GLASS

Strictly speaking, this is a vodka cocktail. However, the addition of the apple brandy and apple juice transforms a simple vodka martini into an Appletini. It's a modern, fruity cocktail known for its vibrant green colour and crisp, sweet, tangy flavour.

YOU WILL NEED

37.5ml vodka

30ml Calvados (apple brandy)

37.5ml apple juice

7.5ml fresh lemon juice

7.5ml simple syrup (see page 17)

Apple slices, to garnish

METHOD

1. Put crushed ice into a glass and set aside to chill.
2. Add the vodka, Calvados, apple juice, lemon juice and simple syrup to a cocktail shaker with ice. Shake until the shaker is cold to touch.
3. Double strain into the glass.
4. Garnish with slices of apple.

BARTENDER TIP

Store clean martini glasses in your freezer so you always have a chilled glass ready for when you need it.

THE LITTLE BOOK OF COCKTAILS

APPLETINI

THE LITTLE BOOK OF COCKTAILS

METROPOLITAN

METROPOLITAN

MAKES: 1.5 LITRES | SERVED IN: COUPE GLASS

This is the classic brandy version of the Metropolitan that dates from the early decades of the 1900s. It's beautifully pinkish in colour but that doesn't distract from its air of sophistication. Its smooth, warming character is perfect if you appreciate classic cocktails.

YOU WILL NEED

60ml brandy

30ml sweet vermouth

2–3 dashes of Angostura bitters

Maraschino cherry, to garnish

METHOD

1. Put a handful of ice in a mixing glass. Add all the liquid ingredients. Stir gently to combine and until chilled.
2. Strain into a glass.
3. Drop in a cherry to garnish.

BARTENDER TIP

Want to pair your Metropolitan with food? The rich flavour of a dark chocolate dessert is a match made in heaven!

STINGER

SERVES: 1 | SERVED IN: OLD FASHIONED GLASS

The Stinger cocktail was perceived to be a high-society drink for New York. Its status was helped by the fact that the millionaire Reginald Vanderbilt had supposedly invented it. With its refreshing mint flavour and smooth finish, the Stinger is often served as an after dinner drink.

YOU WILL NEED

45ml brandy

15ml white crème de menthe

Sprig of fresh mint, to garnish

METHOD

1. Combine the brandy and crème de menthe in a cocktail shaker. Add ice and shake until chilled.
2. Strain into a chilled glass and add some ice cubes.
3. Garnish with a sprig of fresh mint.

BARTENDER TIP

Alternatively, you can serve the Stinger neat, without any ice. This will ensure you can fully enjoy its smooth and refreshing taste.

THE LITTLE BOOK OF COCKTAILS

STINGER

THE LITTLE BOOK OF COCKTAILS

DEPTH BOMB

DEPTH BOMB

SERVES: 1 | SERVED IN: OLD FASHIONED GLASS

Depth bombs were used in the First World War to attack submarines. We can only think that the name of this cocktail therefore refers to the impact of all the brandy in it! Definitely serve this one over ice – as you sip, the ice gradually dilutes the drink to reduce its richness.

YOU WILL NEED

40ml Cognac

40ml Calvados

1 tsp grenadine

2 tsp fresh lemon juice

Lemon slice, to garnish

METHOD

1. Fill a cocktail shaker with ice. Add all the ingredients and shake until chilled.
2. Strain into a glass.
3. Garnish with a slice of lemon and serve with ice.

BARTENDER TIP

When you're making any cocktail, make sure your ice is fresh to ensure your cocktail tastes as good as you intended.

BLACK JACK

SERVES: 1 | SERVED IN: OLD FASHIONED GLASS

This elegant Black Jack balances the deep fruitiness of cherry liqueur with the warmth of brandy and a hint of citrus. The addition of coffee makes it a sophisticated choice if you want a refined and delicious cocktail.

YOU WILL NEED

37.5ml cognac

15ml cherry liqueur

15ml coffee liqueur

30ml cold coffee

Lemon peel twist, to garnish

METHOD

1. Pour all the ingredients into a glass filled with ice.
2. Stir gently to combine and until chilled.
3. Twist the lemon peel over the glass to add a drop of juice.
4. Drop the lemon peel into the glass to garnish.

BARTENDER TIP

If you can't find cherry liqueur, use triple sec instead. While not identical, they are very similar in flavour.

THE LITTLE BOOK OF COCKTAILS

BLACK JACK

THE LITTLE BOOK OF COCKTAILS

DULCE DE TEQUILA

DULCE DE TEQUILA

SERVES: 1 | SERVED IN: COUPE OR MARTINI GLASS

'Dulce de tequila' literally means 'tequila candy', so expect a sweet drink! This is a delicious dessert cocktail that takes its sweetness from the Cointreau and the agave nectar. The tequila adds a bold tone to the overall flavour but the refreshing lime juice balances it all out.

YOU WILL NEED

- 60ml tequila
- 30ml cognac
- 30ml Cointreau (or other orange liqueur)
- 15ml fresh lime juice
- 1 tbsp agave nectar
- Lemon or lime wedge, to garnish

METHOD

1. Fill a cocktail shaker with ice. Pour in the tequila, cognac, Cointreau, lime juice and agave nectar.
2. Shake well to combine and until the shaker is cold to touch.
3. Strain into a glass.
4. Garnish with a wedge of lemon or lime.

BARTENDER TIP

This is a very strong drink that needs sipping rather than rushing. Don't be deceived by its sweetness!

'Too much of anything is bad, but too much Champagne is just right.'

F. Scott Fitzgerald

CHAMPAGNE, WINE & SPARKLES

CHAMPAGNE, WINE & SPARKLES

CONTENTS

Sangria

Mimosa

Kir Royale

Death in the Afternoon

Prince of Wales

ABOUT CHAMPAGNE, WINE AND SPARKLES

Drinks and cocktails that include champagne, wine and sparkles could warrant a book all of their own. They are incredibly versatile as mixers – many classic cocktails can be given a delightful twist with the addition of bubbles, combining the elegance of champagne with the magic of mixology. Champagne and prosecco cocktails are perfect for any celebration or just to treat yourself – you don't need an excuse! Wine cocktails, such as Sangria, provide refreshing options for warmer weather.

(There's a bonus champagne cocktail on page 64 – the French 75.)

SANGRIA

SERVES: 6 | SERVED IN: ANY KIND OF MEDIUM/LARGE GLASS!

Sangria (which means 'blood') is a refreshing Spanish punch made with wine, chopped fruit, and a splash of brandy and orange liqueur. This vibrant and fruity cocktail is perfect for parties and warm weather. Don't get too hung up on the ingredients – sangria is fun so mix it up to your taste.

YOU WILL NEED

- 1 orange, quartered and thinly sliced
- 1 lemon, quartered and thinly sliced
- 2 large apples, peeled, cored and thinly sliced
- 2 tbsp fresh lime juice
- 2 tbsp fresh orange juice
- 100g sugar
- 60ml brandy
- 60ml Grand Marnier (or other orange liqueur)
- 2 bottles of red wine (ideally Spanish)
- 2 litres of club soda, chilled

METHOD

1. Put the sliced fruit in a large jug or container and sprinkle with the sugar and the lime and orange juices. Stir well.
2. Add the brandy and Grand Marnier and leave the fruit to marinate for 3–4 hours.
3. After marinating, pour in the red wine and the soda and stir well.
4. Serve chilled and add ice.

BARTENDER TIP

Classic sangria works best when made with a good quality, young Rioja wine. It has a strong taste with a distinctive aroma of spices.

THE LITTLE BOOK OF COCKTAILS

SANGRIA

THE LITTLE BOOK OF COCKTAILS

MIMOSA

MIMOSA

SERVES: 1 | SERVED IN: CHAMPAGNE FLUTE

The Mimosa cocktail is a light, bubbly drink combining equal parts champagne and chilled orange juice. It's a great choice for brunches, celebrations and toasts. Incredibly simple, you can't go wrong serving this perky classic with its citrus tang and lively bubbles.

YOU WILL NEED

80ml chilled champagne
(or dry sparkling wine or prosecco)

80ml chilled fresh orange juice

METHOD

1. Pour the champagne into a chilled glass.
2. Add the orange juice. Stir gently.
3. And that's it – now serve and enjoy!

BARTENDER TIP

Add a splash of Grand Marnier to make a Grand Mimosa.
Or add a raspberry flavour with Chambord.

KIR ROYALE

SERVES: 1 | SERVED IN: CHAMPAGNE FLUTE

The Kir Royale is one of the most decadent-looking cocktails. It has a deep, rich colour and a delightful balance of bubbly effervescence and fruity sweetness. An elegant drink that enjoys a touch of class and makes a fantastic aperitif.

YOU WILL NEED

1 tbsp crème de cassis

Champagne, chilled, to top up

Fresh blackberry, to garnish

METHOD

1. Pour the crème de cassis into the champagne flute.
2. Top up with the champagne.
3. Garnish with a blackberry. (Or try a strawberry or raspberry.)

BARTENDER TIP

For a variation, swap the champagne for sparkling wine, and the crème de cassis for a raspberry liqueur, such as Chambord. This makes a delicious Kir Impérial.

THE LITTLE BOOK OF COCKTAILS

KIR ROYALE

THE LITTLE BOOK OF COCKTAILS

DEATH IN THE AFTERNOON

DEATH IN THE AFTERNOON

SERVES: 1 | **SERVED IN: CHAMPAGNE FLUTE OR COUPE GLASS**

This cocktail was invented by the American writer Ernest Hemingway in the 1930s. Like its creator, it's a unique drink known for its bold, anise-flavour complexity and effervescent finish. Death in the Afternoon is a potent, yet surprisingly smooth, experience!

YOU WILL NEED

45ml absinthe

120ml champagne, chilled

Twist of lemon peel, to garnish

METHOD

1. Pour the absinthe into a chilled glass.
2. Add the chilled champagne. Stir.
2. Squeeze the lemon peel over the top to add some oily juice and then drop it into the glass.

BARTENDER TIP

When the champagne and absinthe mix, they form a milky, green coloured liquid – don't worry that there are no bubbles. This is the correct result!

PRINCE OF WALES

SERVES: 1 | SERVED IN: COUPE GLASS

Cocktails don't come more regal than this. It is believed that the Prince of Wales was invented by THE Prince of Wales (later to be King Edward VII) after a trip to the US in 1860. Try this one if you like your cocktails spicy, bubbly, bitter, sweet and sour – basically, if you can't make your mind up!

YOU WILL NEED

- 30ml champagne, chilled
- 1 dash Angostura bitters
- 45ml rye whiskey
- ¼ tsp maraschino cherry liqueur
- 1 small piece of pineapple
- 1 tsp simple syrup (see page 17)
- Lemon twist, or pineapple wedge, to garnish

METHOD

1. In a mixing glass, stir together the syrup, bitters, whiskey, liqueur and pineapple.
2. Pour the ingredients from the mixing glass into a cocktail shaker filled with crushed ice. Shake well until the shaker is cold to touch.
3. Strain into a glass and top up with the champagne. Garnish with a lemon twist or pineapple wedge.

BARTENDER TIP

Using bourbon instead of rye whiskey in this recipe will give you a slightly sweeter and fuller flavour.

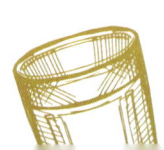

THE LITTLE BOOK OF COCKTAILS

PRINCE OF WALES

'We should all believe in something, and I believe it's time for another shot of tequila.'

Justin Timberlake

TEQUILA

TEQUILA

CONTENTS

Margarita

Tequila Sunrise

Dead Man's Handle

See also Long Iced Tea (page 60)
and Dulce de Tequila (page 126).

ABOUT TEQUILA

Tequila is a distilled spirit made from the blue agave plant. It is mainly produced in the area surrounding the city of Tequila in the Mexican state of Jalisco. This iconic Mexican beverage has a rich history dating back to the Aztec civilization, which fermented the agave plant to produce a precursor to modern tequila. The production process involves harvesting the agave piñas, baking them to convert starches to sugars, fermenting the juice and distilling it. Enjoyed neat, in cocktails or as a shot with salt and lime, tequila's versatile and punchy character has made it hugely popular all over the world.

MARGARITA

SERVES: 1 | SERVED IN: OLD FASHIONED GLASS

The Margarita combines tequila, lime juice and triple sec, balancing the tang of citrus with the boldness of the tequila. It's a refreshing choice whether served on the rocks, frozen or straight up.

YOU WILL NEED

½ wedge of lime

½ tbsp coarse salt, for rim of the glass

60ml blanco tequila

30ml triple sec (e.g. Cointreau)

22.5ml fresh lime juice

Slice of lime, to garnish

METHOD

1. Run the lime wedge around the rim of a glass and then dip the glass in the salt. Set aside.
2. Pour the tequila, triple sec and lime juice into a cocktail shaker. Fill with ice and shake until thoroughly chilled.
3. Strain into the salted glass and add fresh ice cubes.
4. Garnish with a slice of lime and serve.

BARTENDER TIP

The better the quality of the tequila, the better your Margarita will taste. Budget tequila brands can be quite harsh so it's worth spending as much as you can afford.

THE LITTLE BOOK OF COCKTAILS

MARGARITA

THE LITTLE BOOK OF COCKTAILS

TEQUILA SUNRISE

TEQUILA SUNRISE

SERVES: 1 | SERVED IN: COLLINS OR HURRICANE GLASS

The Tequila Sunrise is a vibrant cocktail that gets its name from its stunning colour range. It was created in the 1930s and became popular in the 1970s thanks to the Eagles' song of the same name. Known for its refreshing taste and eye-catching presentation, this is a firm summer favourite.

YOU WILL NEED

50ml blanco tequila

100ml fresh orange juice

1 tbsp triple sec (e.g. Cointreau)

20ml grenadine

Orange slice and maraschino cherry, to garnish

METHOD

1. Fill a glass with ice. Pour in the tequila, orange juice and triple sec. Stir gently to mix.
2. Slowly pour over the grenadine and wait until it sinks to the bottom of the glass.
3. Garnish with an orange slice and a maraschino cherry.

BARTENDER TIP

Always add the grenadine last and don't stir the drink before serving. This ensures you keep the sunrise layers intact!

DEAD MAN'S HANDLE

SERVES: 1 | SERVED IN: POCO GRANDE GLASS

This is a bold cocktail known for its heady mix of flavours. If you like a strong, smooth and well-balanced cocktail that's easy to make, try this. The orgeat syrup adds a sweet and nutty flavour. It's a refreshing drink that packs a punch!

YOU WILL NEED

45ml blanco tequila

15ml Aperol

15ml lime juice

15 ml orgeat syrup (made with almonds, not suitable if you have a nut allergy)

METHOD

1. Combine all the ingredients in a cocktail shaker filled with ice.
2. Shake well until the shaker is cold to touch.
3. Strain into a glass with ice.

BARTENDER TIP

If you want to make your Dead Man's Handle a little drier and les sweet, simply halve the amount of orgeat syrup you use.

THE LITTLE BOOK OF COCKTAILS

DEAD MAN'S HANDLE

'As you get older, the hangovers get really bad ...
I had to make a choice, and I chose mornings.'
Anne Hathaway

MOCKTAILS

MOCKTAILS

CONTENTS

Nojito

Pink Grapefruit Fizz

Shirley Temple

Virgin Piña Colada

Amaretto Sour mocktail

ABOUT MOCKTAILS

These days, any cocktail bar will offer a range of non-alcoholic cocktails – 'mocktails' – on their menu. If you don't drink, don't want to drink or are driving, why should you miss out on the wonderful flavours that cocktails have to offer? Some mocktails are inventions in their own right and others are clever twists on their alcoholic relative, offering a similar taste experience but without the risk of a hangover.

NOJITO

SERVES: 1 | SERVED IN: COLLINS OR HIGHBALL GLASS

A crisp mix of lime and mint, this Nojito is an alcohol-free version of the rum-based Mojito cocktail. It looks almost identical and is as equally delicious and refreshing on the taste buds.

YOU WILL NEED

10 mint leaves

30ml fresh lime juice

30ml simple syrup (see page 17)

Sparkling water, to top up

Slices of lime, to garnish

Sprig of mint, to garnish

METHOD

1. Place the mint leaves and lime juice in a glass. Muddle them for around one minute.
2. Add the simple syrup. Stir well.
3. Top up the glass with the sparkling water and stir again.
4. Garnish with the slices of lime and a sprig of mint.

BARTENDER TIP

For a fruity twist, garnish with additional seasonal fruits – watermelon, strawberries and peach all work well.

THE LITTLE BOOK OF COCKTAILS

NOJITO

THE LITTLE BOOK OF COCKTAILS

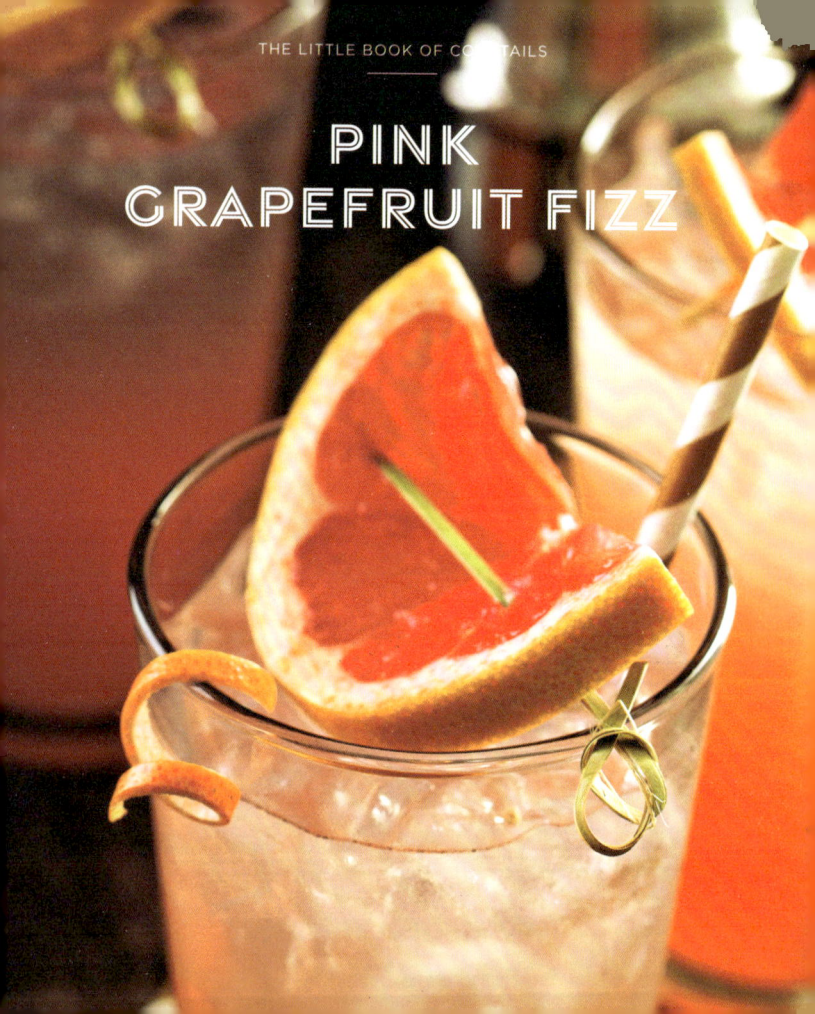

PINK GRAPEFRUIT FIZZ

PINK GRAPEFRUIT FIZZ

SERVES: 8 | SERVED IN: HURRICANE GLASS

This is a refreshing and vibrant cocktail that combines the tart and slightly bitter flavour of pink grapefruit juice with the bubbles of soda water. It's a light, crisp drink making it perfect for summer parties and hot, sunny days. Expect citrusy tanginess with a hint of sweetness.

YOU WILL NEED

350ml pink grapefruit juice

100ml simple syrup (see page 17)

1.25l soda water, chilled

1 pink grapefruit, peeled and sliced

METHOD

1. Put the grapefruit juice and simple syrup in a large jug. Stir to combine.
2. Add the soda water and stir again.
3. Before serving, add the grapefruit slices and a handful of ice cubes.

BARTENDER TIP

Mix up mocktail taste elements – sweet, sour, bitter – in the same way you would in an alcoholic cocktail to balance it out. Experiment!

SHIRLEY TEMPLE

SERVES: 1 | SERVED IN: COLLINS GLASS

The Shirley Temple is probably one of the first and most well-known mocktails. It's a sweet and fizzy drink that combines ginger ale with a splash of grenadine, served over ice. With its bright red colour, this drink is fun for all ages to enjoy.

YOU WILL NEED

15ml grenadine

7.5ml fresh lime juice

150ml ginger ale, chilled

Lime slice and a maraschino cherry, to garnish

METHOD

1. Fill a glass with ice cubes.
2. Pour in the grenadine and lime juice. Stir.
3. Top the glass up with the ginger ale. Gently stir to combine all the ingredients.
4. Garnish with a slice of lime and a maraschino cherry.

BARTENDER TIP

For a bigger hit of ginger, use ginger beer rather than ginger ale. You can also use lemonade or soda water (which will let the flavours of the grenadine stand out more).

THE LITTLE BOOK OF COCKTAILS

SHIRLEY TEMPLE

THE LITTLE BOOK OF COCKTAILS

VIRGIN PIÑA COLADA

VIRGIN PIÑA COLADA

SERVES: 2 | SERVED IN: POCO GRANDE/ PIÑA COLADA GLASS

This Virgin Piña Colada is so delicious, you won't miss the alcohol one bit. It has all the creaminess and summer vibes of the alcoholic version, but can be enjoyed by all the family. You can also use fresh pineapple, but buying frozen chunks is far less labour intensive and it's still packed full of flavour.

YOU WILL NEED

- 250g frozen pineapple chunks
- 60g ice
- 175ml unsweetened pineapple juice
- 175ml unsweetened coconut milk
- 2 tbsp brown sugar
- Fresh pineapple wedges

METHOD

1. Put the pineapple chunks and ice in a blender.
2. Add the pineapple juice, coconut milk and brown sugar. Blend into a purée.
3. Pour into glasses.
4. Garnish with fresh pineapple wedges.

BARTENDER TIP

If you prefer a more coconut-y piña colada, just add more coconut milk. If you prefer pineapple, simply add more frozen pineapple in place of ice cubes.

AMARETTO SOUR MOCKTAIL

SERVES: 1 | SERVED IN: OLD FASHIONED GLASS

Sweet, smooth and the perfect way to round off the day. This mocktail has all the sharp and nutty flavours of the classic Amaretto Sour, without the alcohol. Enjoy on a warm summer's evening.

YOU WILL NEED

100ml pineapple juice

50ml lemon juice

½ egg white

10ml syrup from cocktail cherries

A few drops of almond extract (not suitable if you have a nut allergy)

Cocktail cherries to garnish

METHOD

1. Put the pineapple juice, lemon juice, egg white, cherry syrup and almond extract into a cocktail shaker. Shake vigorously until the egg white has turned the mixture pale and frothy.
2. Add a handful of ice and stir until the shaker is cold to touch.
3. Pour into a glass.
4. Garnish with cocktail cherries.

BARTENDER TIP

Give your Amaretto Sour Mocktail an alternative twist by adding a dash of grenadine or orange syrup.

THE LITTLE BOOK OF COCKTAILS

AMARETTO SOUR MOCKTAIL

MIXING NOTES